Co:ma,to'se

Also by Devanshi Khetarpal

Welcome To Hilltop High

Co:ma,to'se

Devanshi Khetarpal

Illustrations by Ashwin Pandya

PARTRIDGE
A Penguin Random House Company

To order additional copies of this book, contact
Partridge India
000 800 10062 62
orders.india@partridgepublishing.com

www.partridgepublishing.com/india

Contents

For my parents and the wind that doesn't shake the grass

"That you are here- that life exists and identity,
That the powerful play goes on, and you may contribute a verse."

-Walt Whitman, 'O Me! O Life', *Leaves of Grass* (1892)

Acknowledgements

Without the presence of these people in my life, this poetry collection would not have turned out. First and foremost, I would like to thank my parents, Dr. Rajan Khetarpal and Dr. Arneet Arora for being the light in my world. Thanks to my family and friends both in India and overseas for their affection and kindness. Although it would be completely unexpected of me, I would like to express my love for my friends including Ishita Bhatnagar, Arushi Sharma, Anmol Agrawal, Mili Jain, Manvi Jain, Zahra Ahmed, Simarpreet Kaur Oberoi, Vidushi Tiwari and Manasvi Sharma for preventing me from getting forever lost in poetry.

All my teachers at St. Joseph's Convent have encouraged me to write and pursue my dream. Without them and the support given to me by the respected Principal, Sr. Lilly, the staff and my well-wishers, I would not have been able to do such an endeavour. I am forever indebted to my institution for building me up and helping me achieve whatsoever I have.

I am grateful to David Benedictus, my Creative Writing teacher at Oxford Prep Experience 2013. His teaching and guidance has helped me to blossom. His words are of immeasurable value for me.

Needless to say, everyone has a kindred spirit. I would like to thank Trivarna Hariharan, who is acquainted well with my poetry and has taught me a great deal.

A special thanks to Chrys Salt for her useful suggestions before the publishing process. Special thanks to Mr. Ashwin Pandya, the 'Illustrator-for-keeps'. A special thanks to everyone at Partridge for their generosity and for working so efficiently on this project.

Pinafore

Accentuated baguettes lie on taffeta robes where the holly
cocks its head from the fog rolling uphill.

Six fingered grass walls sweep like piano keys over columbine
facsimiles and sciamachy.

In Inglenook's corner, the clock says tick-tock when the coronas
sing an aubade to the balderdashes and popping flingshoots.

Aerosols and gizmos pass the numbing curtains, cornices
yet in disrepair, with the prints of a New England daddy.

Tombstones and rarebit mingled over the campanile's growl
a-receding, dreary dust jackets tied with killer stoles and
flashy knives- all painting the frills of my 1999 pinafore.

Roses And Thorns

Roses of dormant silence
itch under trimmed patches
of my elbow, hidden amid
vacant scabs from yesteryear.

Their thorns dream about
dandelions sweeping the surface with
the cold desiccated chinook in my undone garden.

Reference

Those expurgated days
dangled like body fat
over the purlieu of my hometown.

We left our food
lolling in dirt
lest the wind
would be kind enough to burn it into ashes

and give us a slow chance to die.

When we saw
butterflies debilitating nectar, we kissed
their lips to inhale the motifs in their wings
and tucked them on the underside
of our tongues. When rest

grinded us, we stayed calm but
vowed to quell the melodies

clogged in our throats.

Our nerves would rise like sand dunes,
merging our knuckles with our skin
to see how tips of our fingers
waltzed, if we were to sleep.

Tunnel

"Cry, dear." When the last voice
will hurl civilization, we'll stop
passing exegeses to and fro the tunnel.
The wind will remain stagnant over your
window sill.

I'll throw a dove into the mist so it may sit and
draw your portrait and when
its eyes are knackered of your beauty,
I'll ask it to squat by an ant hill
and watch Saturn cave in on
our horizon, hanging like a coat in a giant cabinet,
lying in the incompleteness of stardust.

Somewhere

Somewhere we all lose our self in the
smallness of our names. Our skins open
to unravel our entrails,

mobbed with the precision of the croissants
lying famished on the table. While we turn
our spirits on wet pillows, we see chrysanthemums
swallowing frills to worship the sky.

But in the place named somewhere so
unimaginatively by someone, we seek
succour from the young fruits that reach
our spirits while we snooze under the
worn-out apparel of the busiest roads.

Appetite

I try to nudge my hand,
assuaging those strokes advancing from the
prie-dieu over the bleached shadows of the tsetses,
looking upon your slouched shoulder like a cliff
dropping from the hinge of my door.

My hands try to cut your face like beanstalks.
You subtly garrote your upper lips
to stitch them within the dominions of your spoon.

Sometimes extracting ruby glass and banderoles
from the overlapping cross nets of my skin,
you trim them like strudels and stars
that mingle into daylight when they
surmount the winding staircase to my right.

While Uncle Albert whiffed the
snow for his keys, you were
infatuated with the virtue of infidelity. An hour
later, I killed the crickets somnambulating
under your loafers.

You kneecap inhales the ground
occupied by the ferns. Rocks slither
during a landslide. Your knees burn the
broadcasts that yelped like mongrels when we took birth.

Devanshi Khetarpal

They have corybantic wealth kept under
their tongues when they harangue about the geography
of our music- silent as the coming of death.
When they pass detestable fritters, they look
at you and sigh. I don't know why.

Tuck Shop

Tossing our heads over
cold mosaic-like winged grasses,
does our heart carry our gibberish onus when
we see all the sand die
beneath our subconscious earthly sins?
Perhaps the hours hover

as we whoosh our eyesight
akin to that precocious gush of wind,
blowing past the thrushes to write
its genteel banter all over the papery fog,
hollering in our intestines.

Maybe our cries are too loud- too shrill
like the world where it stands on the derriere
of our twitched palms while our neighbourhood
buttons its shirts and ruches them inside.
Somewhere, we are lovers
who are wide awake when the tuck shop
is open and near or the sun buys a
siesta for its fallowed price in the
depth of an undergrowth.

Masquerades

I quaff masquerades of dust down
my throat, constricting my flesh
into slightly saturated bottlenecks.

Curiosity branches high, swearing
in voices that scale the mountains. My
bowtie throws back its shards at me,
almost caving in a burrow
lined with regalia.

Blinded Walls

Looking at the blinded walls,
shrouded by thin yarns-
branched wide and rooted deep,
entwining into passageways of
glowing barricades and hollow winds-

I pass like a
traveller's succinct whistle down the
conflagration of mountain verdure immersed in
the lark's song.

I hum a thousand songs with
one beat,
one chord,
one note.

I glide as a child trying to
catch the smothering sparks of my identity.
Not a single toast of the air has
passed untouched between nuanced flesh.

When I crack the blinded walls,
I stitch my own footsteps through
barren cloaks in silenced couloirs.

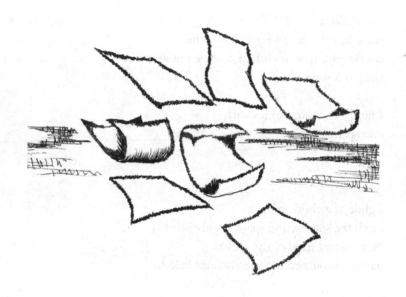

Staining The Silent Lobby

Paper dribbles
across the
lobby.

Silence
soars high
to trap
flying language.

Behind
tiny lines,
hearts
stain.

Downpour

The tinted
tumbler has
snapped
your silhouette.

I can see you
bending over
the foyer,
your head
in disguise.

The scarlet rays
have inhaled your
eyeballs like
coffee beans
triturated and tossed
onto the marble floor.

There is a
stained floor,
where all that is left to
see are boulders
of different hues
snatched from the
azure seabed.
A welkin has
lost its cloudy ships,
turbulent tides
and dreams of
soaring vaulted roofs.

Dry Skin

A Monday
was gleaming
on the horizon, passing
into the blurred flexures of paper airplanes.

My two fingers-
haunched on my knuckles-
simply swept
and tore away.

I lied on the beds
of those little
sunken valleys,
I'd been told not to tread upon.

He'd turned me into
a tissue roll of
red, steaming,
blood-glazed surfaces. He's too kind.

In A Lifetime

Times clip,
finally.

Poison breath
brings tears.

War of words,
pious.

Unquiet colours
moved.

Times,
quiet.

Goodbyes tossed
in the view.

Till Roses Grew In Ashtrays

Till roses grew in ashtrays,
the cigars
simply withered
in the centre of the breeze.
I look at the porcelain sink,
contemplating
if that is the place
I come from.

Sometimes our words
erupt in the silence of
our hearts, ticking away
and ending us
bluntly. We all awoke from
the suburbs of forbidden woods, the
places of no escape.

I push
the bricks-
standing skyward over
skyward-

hitting my head against the air.
The bottom
of the ocean
was fast asleep
on the day
when I saw
my first heartbeat

ebbing

into seas of comatose.

Saturday

Sitting through the years
after all the folly,
threads have woven my
unanimous heartiness into the soft linen
running under my feet. It's
dauntless,
avid and
young like the shunned music.

Redline

A disappearance
of mangroves

from cities,

villages.

Expanding displacement
is no grim display

on the redline.

Three Pilgrims Can

Foreign religion
doesn't shine
in the sun.

Three pilgrims can
wipe that century

with their
fatal vows.

Disapproval

Near Florida,
a child dismisses
friends of

the stormy spotlight
working through music
on

a New Year's eve.

Crusader

When a world
scraps ashes,

a crusader

invites everyone
with helmets and
shatters of laconic fever

back home to enter the innards of time.

Realisation follows.

Candlelight

The candles
on the table
were shining.
At times, they
stopped. The
flame was

a cluster,
a sack of fireflies.

Signature

Today, I found the words I left adrift in 1947
in the swerve of your signature.

I sat squinting as its tarnishing
silhouette started turning into a colossal
doodle of your philistine pencil upon a
thin wafer sheet with ragged edges.

Its elucidation was spread over
like a defensive barbed wire that runs from
this capital to that capital.

Our cities and the newly drawn lines took my heart away like
a gust of some mild storm from the dark past that
comes sprinting over, enveloping its hands
around my recent realities
and turns my present tense into a browning effulgence.

I am rowing my ship. My masts have
overlooked the waves for an eternity.
I come back, straining all the way to
get my shoulders coil behind my back
and row back to the shore, pretending to be the noble oarsman.

Devanshi Khetarpal

I found your signature,
resting under a cork,
sleeping under the algid afghans
of a glass bottle. Your lips
have been imprinted on it. Stamped in such a manner
that no sun or moon will ever be able to
choke it to death.

Novel

Give me a serious story.

Without a baron
and
no Shakespeare
and
no pure bonds.

Life sets soon-
so soon,
so quick,
so sudden.

Why journey?

Betty Black

Her silver crowns
turn tenebrous
in waters,
fetched from the
veils of hell.

The little game of croquet
that we played in the
slight imitation of the monocle went
dry in the winds, drunk in the
acidity of the dew's last tear which
went blue in the corner whites.

Hands waver
and brush

the music,

the skyline turning into a cicatrix
while we carefully flop
swears into the purity of
our lethal hymns.

Mouths turn
into circles,
saying words
of first farewells.

Our fingers
enclosed packages
addressed to the streets
where we lost paperbound lives
in the gloomy clouds
of charcoal drawn on the
graphite

by a child
born of the
earth's turpitude.

Forgiveness

I took a step forward
Until the platform
Soaked me.

Soaked me in
its black murals.

Flight

On the thinned ball made from
the descent of the eventide, we united
our laces and saw the tiny orts of
stars and broken moons reach the soil.
There, mayblob had blossomed from
freezing ferns as they trembled under a
dark sea which engulfed the firmament.

While we stretched our footsteps
on Magpie Lane, to go beyond
doors filled with surreal
possibilities- locked since the first leaf fell
on consecrated grasses that break the swan's feather
while it fleets on the Cherwell.

We hear odd
chimneys and kettles that have been blazing
on our misplaced candelabras and calendars since the
	beginning of
a third meal in this century. And then to see,
cinders getting lost among jewels and to
keep quiet when we know the world around is
a true illusion.

We keep not our shadows and not all
those balls near. They're far off. They've gone
beyond London into a place we know exists
but know not exactly the latitude. All we know is
that the midnight sun carved from ferocious
blinds of our twice occurring deaths will once kiss the west
    coastline.

When Jamie held a hand under
that banyan tree which stands resting on the
Fellows' Garden, he doesn't quite see the barricade
which pronounces its gaudy leaflessness. On its branches,
the fluttering destitution of a partridge learns
to fly among the cardboard castles of Henley.

At a place where Big Ben led us, we
saw under a flight of perfumes that penetrated
the walls, how our cannikins filled
with elixir that jerkily kept us awake.

If we ever saw that deluge of obscured light,
on an unaccustomed terra firma,
we'd notice how obscene the piano's
melodies have turned.

Lungs

I was blind like a
thousand petty arms of the
sea holding the waves.

My ship has seen the
masts, the winds, the waters and
the skies for too long.

I do not know at
all how my ship coughs when it's
lungs are asphyxiated.

Locked

Your heart
is throbbing on
the edges of my desk.

You'd better lock
it in the closet.

Train

I got
off the
11.45 train.

I haven't seen a
man without a tattoo
on his arms.

A taxi has finally pulled up.

His arm is clean,
his name is John.

Just like I anticipated.

Three Petals (And A Bee)

In that billet doux sent from a territory
of bygone centuries, crushed old leaves
of potted ambiguity got trapped betwixt the gentle
pigments of a handful of parched diaries.

Among those instances, one emerged
from the desks of the manse that we adorned
with silver, cut carefully from the empty moccasins
of our memoirs. That one instance where it burnt itself
and then shed its ashes on our aligned dinner plates,
hurriedly ransacked the hanging daybreak, leaving
us to starve and commit scores of proud sanctimony- raw as the
harsh note of the crow spread across mammoth expanses.

From your fifth overstretched syllable, the second instance of
that unfavourable night awoke when we played jazz in the
      summer
of Essex. When a Derby daddy arrived to meet a Yorkshire
      daddy,
you leapt across the cries left as a residue on your
      primogeniture-
a rug which stands aloof from the world yet half a metre in it.
Our dictators- the ones that float on the back of our
      spines- sometimes
swallow our tears as they gush down our loose skin
and churn it into the cheese manufactured in milky way.

Devanshi Khetarpal

The third petal fell like a shaft of the artificial light of the
sun at midday. My clock has been suffering from
indigestion. When the midnight arrives, it falls to the floor
baking under the stiff hazards of our loafers. It pins
dozens of glass windows on its ankles and then attempts
to cycle down the besmeared ethnicities of the half-lighted
venations of the leaves.

When the bee arrived, I looked into his eyes and let
my damp breath soak them. So we eloped
far from the world that we called our own and coiled
in a blanket made with the losing phonetics that sank
deep under the arches.

Tuesday

Truth
unfurls.
Eating
stuffed
dinosaurs
as they were
yours.

Jolly

You share the oubliette with a maniac
you never expected to meet in the falsehood of your dreams
that plummeted on the dock of the origami ship,
stepping into monochromatic worlds
where all you can get lost in is your own fur-
estranged from a world that accounted for its adjective.

Keep yourself to yourself. Greet and wring me.
Don't be surprised if my aspects are much too puerile to behold
the truth you carry in the craters of your guts.

If you imagine the world becoming heaven's slaughterhouse,
you are right. You see their bereaved blood
dripping on our pavements, proliferating underneath the curls
      of asphalt.

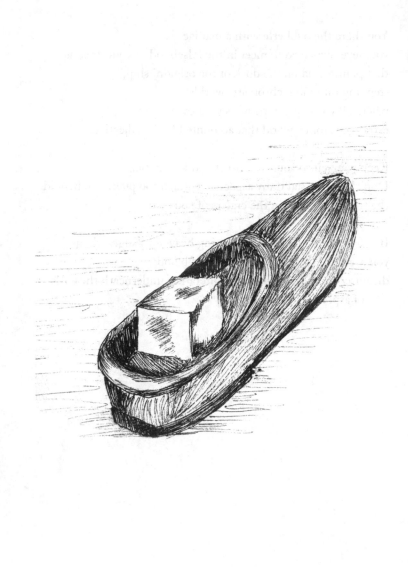

Ice

I have kept the ice cubes in my shoe.
They feel alive in its motionless sobriety.

Sometimes, we let the ravenous ice
bristle over our ecru hearts and letting a
gelatinous shell of audacity and bathos step
in, we start to live as if we are entreating them with the
monolithic dust that escapes the canyons of
our flesh.

Dreams

There are those who are perfect,
who were not thrust with clocks
in their netted penalties.

Time has a good sense of humour.
We know it since we've seen it
ascertain its immortality over the ages.

This spring, which skips the air
of all that is true, will not
sequester itself behind the blinds.

Those blossoms, whose feet writhed
against the wafts will stay there, pinned onto
the canvas of our fluid gesticulation.

Sunshine, climb upon us! We hold
no grudges against your haughty pauses
since the fray of December. You are the demigod

with your queer habiliments like that of a
woodwork drool. Pass your candle like
a saturated wall into the coarseness of our
dreams.

Illegitimacy

The peak of justice exhumes
confetti upon illegitimate mistrals.

The blindness of the leaves makes us think
thrice, causing us to revel in fits

of absolute deaths that efface as we grow
to survive- our days pullulating towards the descent.

Do we lose our bodies in the paleness and the
moistened abuttals of the leaves, sweeping

the law upon us to be worthy of
appraisal. None have seen the frights, the sounds or

the rafts of cabinets filled with adventures.

Corrosion

We want to see exactly how you corrode.
Your palms may not fit in the peek holes
you've left for supper, too timeless to be consumed
by the fraction of séance that we take in with
every break in the air's floorboard.

Voyage

There is a crutch which
upholds my voice. I can see
it flow with my sound.

Before I sink, will
you let me say my last words?
That is not a vow.

The Morning After

I

Day 24400

With the hinterland crisscrossing the admissible waters,
there's only a hint of what was left in the tin burette.
Is there something that we may call our religious
mortality, if not the dearth of our free-falling ways?
In the town across the bayou, there is a thaumaturge whose
eyes plunge into the freshness of our fates to
present the lantern we may have to carry on the train back to
your residence where you keep your shoes intact in their
symmetrical holiness, lined with the blessings of tawny
skills- too shrewd to keep us awake any longer.

II

Day 24401

Gazing at your wilful eyes and armed scales,
I am bound to think that the harp is like a patrol.
Aunt Martha uses the wise garrison to keep her
chutzpah wrecked and reeking in the crises of today's
backbones. The sun forks its notes high up in the mist,
scaling the ineffable fraternity of our ploughs. Like yours, her
hand only reveals the youth drying up on the subservient
plurality of our wastefulness. But Aunt Martha was different,
much different from the woman who painted my walls and
bled her sins in titillating strokes thereafter.

III

Day 24402

Sometimes a shaggy rug can upturn our manifold
spirits into the frailty of guttural metaphors. We should
let ragged edges cut our esplanades to make way for the
timid pedestrian to undo his arms and let them sink into the
estuary. Your death only prevails like atheism, making me do
    away
with the bitter aesthetics of spirituality and believe in the
conceited disbelief of your fumes as they pace the earth
that runs east and revolves south on the chippers of our
egresses. Your capsized sleeping posture dooms the
restlessness of your winking eyes and makes you smell the
    flocculent pillows.

Leaving Stonehenge

The grass beleaguers under the thin stalks of
   my body, lying in the gigantic openness that
      pulverizes the stones placed on the blades' mantelpiece.

Boulders have lied in the obsolescence of this juncture,
   fit to be the masters of my prestidigitation- bedraggled
      and restricted under cocoons of syrupy amber dropped by
      the sun.

I've learnt my mistakes and the art of rectifying
   those which aren't mine entirely. A fly can lift its feet
      to put kibosh on all the soothsaying that lies in this
      wilderness.

It's hard to believe the myth that walks silently in the
   tasteful whisks of separation. I'd only seen half the balls
      row out of the lakes of my loquacious proclivities that are
      to live forever.

Covered Market

I phoned Jack six minutes ago just to question
how it felt to be guillotined. He was sitting with me

on Table 6 at Brown's. We all knew very well that our
twinning times were brimming against the tiles we'd

been working hard to paint with soot. We were drowning in the
seabed of coffee. Then, Jack looked up. He shoved a criminal
glance to a lady with a pink umbrella and a cocktail dress put on
    her ample waist. Hours
later, he got married to her. I didn't ask why because he was still

checking the time to find an answer. I had nothing to do after
he left. The stores were closing down and behind the counter,
people had started counting.

Played two truths and a lie with spoon.

I cinched the base of my broken demitasse, staring at the foamy
innards and the scent of my mouth that I had brushed brusquely
    against

it. My footsteps, however, started to step out of those
    quincunxes of coffee.
When John was guillotined, I wanted to know how it was like
to smash your head against two faces of goodness. I was next in
    line.

That's a teaspoonful of it.

The Crosswords Of Fire

Born from
farewell
flames.

From the
dry
game

of the
fire's
winds.

Leave.

Shrouded.

From the realms of
rich,
old,
magical

colour.

A Game Of Lacrosse

It is five o' clock.

Reaching the brink of nothing

in the lacrosse winds.

Play Time

And it was play time.
The eagles came out too soon.
Perhaps, I was wrong.

Holly

So much for the love
of shimmering aspects,
the grass blades turned black.

Little drops of sun
made me see
the plant

losing

the name of

olive green.

A Name For Bodies

Peterson, John;
Freeman, Ted
are dancing.

Kensington, Daniella;
Jones, Sarah
are living.

Eliot, William;
Francis, Nicholas
are dead.

Moore, Samantha;
Davies, Daniel
are praying.

Field, Christopher;
Miller, Mary
are hoping.

And I
am running
out of names.

me
nes for
ne bodies.
I want names
for
everybodies,
somebodies,
anybodies,
nobodies.

Tomorrow will arrive.

The Boys Like White Balloons

There is only a star in the sky. But it's the first one that we've
    seen after
a millennium has gone by- drifting away into the nothingness and
the atomicity of the past. I've launched several folds of skin into
    the
loops of jargon, but there's only two closed eyes that I've
    received.

A ball of wool and a rocking chair that leans on a grandfather
    clock-
that's all we saw on the floor on Christmas morning. Several
    centuries ago,
fifteen boys had come in with their blankets and settled in the
    cellar
where they died in the arms of whom we call the clippers of our
    ruefulness.

They wore those ragged linen trousers so proudly that we began
    to question the
frivolity of our crimes. None with sagging skin has set foot on
    this town. It would
be unnatural if suddenly a bit of beer would fall on the grass and
    kill it. I'm sure
this time your teeth will only catch and possibly loosen up
    because I haven't yet

...ven Jack for the vibe of pain that he passed onto my ankles.
   I created eternal moonlight

...n a tree whose leaves were only supposed to mingle with the
   fences that

we set ablaze. It was the summer of 1945 and I was sitting on
   the worst park bench

trying to hear it sing for a fleet of chrysanthemums. But those
   boys always

liked white balloons. In your tub, I could see soft threads
   mingle with the sky

which keeps gazing upon me. Inside your closed eyes, you can
   encapsulate the

wings of kisses that the earth passes from the fringes of its
   forehead. The meadows

are the ones with the black balloons but you've still got your fur
   to mend.

In Ink

If on a winter's night a traveller,
waiting for the barbarians
to kill a mockingbird.

Desert,
disgrace,
are a thousand splendid suns.

Midnight's children
amid the city of Djinns
are sitting in the room on the roof.

Pride and prejudice,
sense and sensibility
are a clockwork orange.

A house for Mr. Biswas,
opposite mansfield park
in the sea of poppies.

Hullabaloo in the guava orchard,
brings war and peace,
crime and punishment.

Dropping names
in the afterparty
on the fourth of June.

The masque of Africa
taking measure for measure

midsummer night's dream.

in the age of iron,
with wings of fire
and ignited minds.

A walk to remember
on return to the hundred acre wood
at breaking dawn.

Co.

Breakfast In The Park

No two angels are alike in bunk beds. No water is the same blue.
No weeds look the same if they are cut. No perfection is ever as
    correct as it seems.

But stained glass always holds itself true against the sunlight.
    Colours mount
the sunken walls. And the view across the bridge doesn't change
    as frequently
as our hatefulness. Only the still waters are brimming in a gap
    and only the trees
are stooping lower to act as bait.

Each time we turn our backs, another flower blossoms in the
    snowfall.
Another cloak wriggles out of the cupboard and is tossed on the
    floor
or sometimes, a sneezing car.

It's the breakfast in the garden that hasn't changed. People
    mismatch their shoes
and leave the rest for the sky to decide. All of us are living
    underground but we're
falling on the surface. All of us are going downstairs.

Faucets

That day, he was the
only one passing the
thoroughfare with a
fleet of running faucets
in his arms.

At that very minute,
I cried. I always had a
certain connubial love
for faucets but all I can
see, at the moment, are his
footprints- bedraggled and
hollering in the
slightness of the day.

Allochthonous

I see
brown daylight
taking three
steps down
the staircase.

It trips over
my skin.
Boils it
to the ignoble
tears my heart
sheds too
often.

It makes my eyes
burst into
clouds.

I see bearded walls
caged under deprived
touches.

I am a good
wrangler
now that I own
words that speak although
I have no skin left.

ose coverings,
ere feeble.
They simply wound
themselves
over my
pulsating half-full arteries
but they never
really dared
to stand
the pitch.

The throb.

My arms were
broken and I was
living on
the awful
poison the
cemeteries usually
made me drink.

I have been
looming over the
pointing,
piercing,
cutting edges
which scissor
their way
through.

The emerald sea
is bouncing atop
my life.

But I,

cannot forget
what those
little jewels
have done.

The light was broken.

It was in discord
to the quadrille.

But it has
snatched me away
and
dragged me
across sands
and
the heather
that is placed
far apart from
where I belong.

I am allochthonous.

The Draught

Her upper lip ceased with the pandemonium. A clump of trees
flooded with the fall's sounds. Tony silently brushed his hair out
   of the view

and crept up to the pillar. Four centuries ago,
one boy had taken the butterflies into the mellowed smells

of beastly heavens. People started arriving with
their sweaters and began to train craters on how to judge
      someone's

toenail. The breaks in the earth, caused by the retreating rubble,
has been filled with warm skin of a colour that belongs to life

and its accursed beginnings.

Sting

A December stings.
Victory to frost shreds,
bang to the fire.

Catching lame ducks
is mean.

Paper Airplanes

I

The cobalt streams underneath the sun
brushed windows. The candelabra remains the same-
unkempt, in ruins- just as you left it.

When you last knocked on that wooden door
with a bouquet of orchids to hand her, you trampled
on her dahlias. You were an old fool, gone berserk

in trying to know how she'd been keeping herself alive
for over two decades.

At 8.05, you slammed the door behind when you
rushed in convoluting steps. I remember the faint hour which
began at 8.06 when she wiped her face clean with

some bed linen and stroked her neck with
your old checked shirt that hung clumsily in a
vertigo, in ruffles behind the door.

The floor was cold. My packed lunch came straight out
of its misery.

III

I came home just to kiss her luscious cheek
for the first time since the dawn had blinded my
French window.

It was salty, struck with the feverish truth of
all that you left behind. Her mouth smelt of the kind of
stuff you'd keep hidden in the cellar.

Just the very thought makes me dizzy while I'm
creating a meadow for myself in her arms.

IV

Daddy, the mistrals come from the south this time-
mismatched with the dimness of the streetlights. It hovers
around her feet while her skin faces its unnerving duress blithely.

She's gone under the white sheets, keeping her
finger still pointing straight towards your pillow. I know it's
strange to speak, to remember, to mumble, to enunciate,

to emphasise, to cry, to think and to sleep in the flexures of
      someone's collar.
But she does it each time she pours herself into your slippers
      when the lights go off.

There are creases in her voice, their music has started to
binge on the beetles that search for serendipity under the bed.

There are a bunch of paper airplanes stoking the fire because
      your
long journey has become a thick residue and her cadaver has
      stopped
jolting against the marble. It lies still.

A Little Boy with Big Feet

Someone's shoe will stop you by the lake.
If you wash a ring in the water, it will only
cause a riot for you to draw a sword
and kill the water out of everyone.

Your hands are already wrinkled and your
heart is already still but living in a land of
silence,
lifelessness.

Once your fourth anniversary is gone by,
you shall forget your name. You'll be thinking
about people you haven't met yet.

Someday, you'll lie just as you did two years ago.
You'll be seated on a throne of ice only to be given away to
the flames.

It's true. Because all of us live that way. We are fed into
the ice or into the fire. Trumpets cross the road to
deliver a farewell song. Only a

dancer with black shoes will be able to save you.

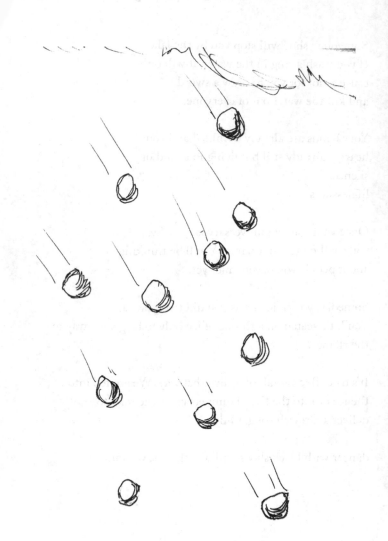

Fishing, Snowfall, Snapping

The snapping snow
brings a mistake.

Shining light
is that half snowfall
for a tin home
without cracked
walls.

Geriatrics

For five months, we spent our lives on the
miserably cold linen in the hospital ward.

We were happy to see our poetics fly off
into the fringes of still beds, sleeping like the

somnambulating winds.

Guilty

There are little feet rustling on
the grass. From the balcony, our tears
halted over our dry bones when we beheld

the finesse of the leaves, scorching
under the furious spasms of the sun trying to
gulp everything down to where the seabed sleeps.

On the wooden bench, you and I
sat silently with our words floating into the
name which was scribbled on it. Our elbows have

managed to scrap the skin and the
clouds have been under curfew in strangers' neighbourhoods
to make way for the criminal heat- waving in frail torrents
     above our halos.

Evolution

The earth careens on glass slates.
We seem to have slipped by the frondescence.
Somewhere deep in the acute imperfection
of time, all the tresses filled with blinding innocence,
bridge into dust.

I remember you sliding under the sand that rested
firmly by my toe- clinching to my weight as if
I was the axis of what lay beneath. What you hold upon
your breath is nothing but the heaving sigh of
an unceasing array of spumescent clouds

which know all that we're bereft of
knowing. Now your gentle teeth
sip the spirit, eject elixir into where
it slowly turns into winding numbers, sleeping
upon the frown of a ruffled skin.

It's hard to maintain symmetry. The symmetry
of that bottled moment that ended so quickly as the beginning
of life, has left me ponderous. Your earthly kiss has been
    covered
by a sheath. It lies locked in a tight corner where I bleed the
    outcries of the moon
when it watched you descend the stars to a world resembling
    speckled ash.

Someone Dies On A Bridge

A triumph was killed too soon to be recalled.
Someone dies on a bridge. Will you ask the
water to freeze or would it rather meander through
the paralysing connotations?

A duck steps aside and the marshy land is simply
too gigantic to spot a cloud. We've lost all
our fraternity in the quarter of a second. There is
still some marmalade left to ponder on.

Whether we slice our lives and wear it like a skirt,
or whether we keep our sentences and use them as
a spoon, it's ruthless attempting to live more than
we're capable of.

Whiskered Clouds

It seems far-fetched to say that the hungry clock ate
a wet tree. The children kept looking at the sea bouncing back
at their feet. A tide's prose is the only foundation
of the sea's poetry when it stars in the drama of the sky.

For twenty years, the children kept their windows open
to see the snow-capped mountains concatenate their peaks
like cups of white coffee. The mountain's bosom takes a breath
in and glaciates the river, glissading strongly across its skin

like a taffeta robe. Children know what the play is. The game
is one where no party acquires a gold spoon and the loss is
    commensurate to
the state of jocund affairs. If a hungry clock and a wet tree
died in the forest, would the children be proud to have seen
their kinsmen turn before the whiskered clouds?

& Bread

Inside, the black walls fall in the
garden. Shadows lean on the crimson air and sing
whatever is left in the autumn leaves. The roof
is shaking while the stillness dances on its
edges.

I asked a fingerbowl how it will cut my life into two.
The blankness of five incisions made me
alive last summer. As I squatted on the grey slate
that covered my death like a dull curtain drawn
on a broken window, I felt

the moon slowly twisting its arms and
setting down, amalgamating with the water.
If that is how I had to die, I'd have the sea rest
and the tides fall underneath their respective
ambiguities and not come close

to my poetry. The coquettish smell of
words conquer the cupboard- the ones that I hope remain,
even when the world has been sucked out of my pockets.

Peregrine

Tongues are braided in beryl. Voices on the chersonese can only
be clenched by fists of rocks. But stoppages come in great lives,
only to write in the gridlines with the certainty of deduction.

Since a levee can make our lives so existentially horizontal, you,
    with
your soft claws now pausing the earth's act, can only influence
half a jar of honey left open in the wilderness, gazing at infinity.

For wordsmiths and hair quaver the exact dimensions
of our fears, we can scarcely trust them to tell us so. Their
    dreams
can be untied far too uncomfortably for us to notice a hand
    waving near

the dim streetlights, bugs hovering in the crossroads of
    sunshine. Even
when the light throws a shadow, it is easy to forget the
    admonition
and consider a principle correct before the shallow chambers of
    sustenance

open themselves to further ado. A fuller view from the
    glass- and
a plumper hand stretches out with pinker lips to come close
to make your scarlet rays hide behind the curtains.

The bend of your neck only preaches the truth snoring
under the wrap's lie. Screams stop the turn of the screw, flying
daggers cross the bridges to enter our hearts and

the only icicle that is left in the dry air can be enough
to unravel the folds of blankets and give us half a rhyme to
live by.

Punnet

It's hard not to think of the beginning once we're
reaching the end. Everything stays. Like the ten walls
on the street which lead to my favourite view.

We all look outside the windows, standing there: hidden. But I
     find the rocks on my
heels and the stars on my forehead. Only the sunrise and sunset
haven't quite drawn themselves on my hands.

The fine lines are a series of truths. We've been blind too.
Someone told me that if I die young, they'll bury me with my
glasses on.

Schatzi

Sherbet shreds and straws fill the visceral
wafts of the deipnosophist. Trees line the avenues and
the drummers roll over the ladies' cloche hats.

Five tabloids are hidden under the palavers
of an ivory table as it shifts a glance to the peaks and
scales a heightened burgundy warfare theory.

Punt

He slipped two crates of gold under my door and finally,
there's a monologue punting on my tummy. Fine legs and
white seas like floating blocks of crystals seize my mind

and a bus-stop is created behind the fringes of
the garden wasps.

Out there, Magdalene is shining in the sky and I can hear
birches screaming somewhere on a hill, too far to be noticed.

Tyranny

When the first hand reached the spotted sky,
all the dead watches stopped ticking. They found
a species that was highly evolved, that needed the passage of
    time
to guide it through the alleys.

What does one expect to hear? The shore's sigh upon the
    mellow
rustiness of the dusty dawn is enough to shun the revolt.
The profundity of what we call eternal discovery,
is the continuance of a small risk.